I0426142

Evaluation of the Sensitivity of Inventory and Monitoring National Parks to Acidification Effects from Atmospheric Sulfur and Nitrogen Deposition

Southeast Alaska Network (SEAN)

Natural Resource Report NPS/NRPC/ARD/NRR—2011/373

T. J. Sullivan
T. C. McDonnell
G. T. McPherson
S. D. Mackey
D. Moore

E&S Environmental Chemistry, Inc.
P.O. Box 609
Corvallis, OR 97339

April 2011

U.S. Department of the Interior
National Park Service
Natural Resource Program Center
Denver, Colorado

The National Park Service, Natural Resource Program Center publishes a range of reports that address natural resource topics of interest and applicability to a broad audience in the National Park Service and others in natural resource management, including scientists, conservation and environmental constituencies, and the public.

The Natural Resource Report Series is used to disseminate high-priority, current natural resource management information with managerial application. The series targets a general, diverse audience, and may contain NPS policy considerations or address sensitive issues of management applicability.

All manuscripts in the series receive the appropriate level of peer review to ensure that the information is scientifically credible, technically accurate, appropriately written for the intended audience, and designed and published in a professional manner.

This report received peer review by subject-matter experts who were not directly involved in the collection, analysis, or reporting of the data. Data in this report were collected and analyzed using methods based on established, peer-reviewed protocols and were analyzed and interpreted within the guidelines of the protocols.

Views, statements, findings, conclusions, recommendations, and data in this report do not necessarily reflect views and policies of the National Park Service, U.S. Department of the Interior. Mention of trade names or commercial products does not constitute endorsement or recommendation for use by the U.S. Government.

This report is available from Air Resources Division of the NPS (http://www.nature.nps.gov/air/Permits/ARIS/networks/acidification-eval.cfm) and the Natural Resource Publications Management website (http://www.nature.nps.gov/publications/nrpm/).

Please cite this publication as:

Sullivan, T. J., G. T. McPherson, T. C. McDonnell, S. D. Mackey, and D. Moore. 2011. Evaluation of the sensitivity of inventory and monitoring national parks to acidification effects from atmospheric sulfur and nitrogen deposition: Southeast Alaska Network (SEAN). Natural Resource Report NPS/NRPC/ARD/NRR—2011/373. National Park Service, Denver, Colorado.

NPS 953/107409, April 2011

Southeast Alaska Network (SEAN)

National maps of atmospheric S and N emissions and deposition are provided in Maps A through D as context for subsequent network data presentations. Maps A and B show county level emissions of total S and total N, respectively, for the year 2002. Map C shows total S deposition and Map D shows total N deposition, again for the year 2002. Regional deposition data are not available for Alaska, but deposition would be expected to be very low throughout most, but not necessarily all, of Alaska.

There are three parks in the Southeast Alaska Network: Glacier Bay (GLBA), Klondike Gold Rush (KLGO), and Sitka (SITK). Only GLBA is larger than 100 square miles.

Total annual S and N emissions, by county, are shown in Maps E and F, respectively, for lands in and surrounding the Southeast Alaska Network. County-level emissions of both S and N within the network were uniformly less than 1 ton per square mile. Point source emissions of SO_2 are shown in Map G. The few point sources, each of which emitted less than 5,000 tons of S per year, were centered around the one population center located in the network. Map H shows point source emissions of oxidized (nitrogen oxides, NO_x) and reduced (ammonia, NH_3) N in this network. There were no N point sources of any magnitude.

Urban centers within the network and within a 300-mile buffer around the network are shown in Map I. There are no urban centers larger than 50,000, and only one larger than 25,000.

Maps J and K are not shown because there are no regional total S or N deposition data for Alaska. There is a near total absence of population centers and point sources.

There are five active NADP/NTN wet deposition monitoring sites in Alaska: Poker Creek, Juneau, Denali National Park, Gates of the Arctic National Park, and Katmai National Park, with data collected since 1980 at Denali and since 1993 at Poker Creek. The other three monitoring sites have been added within the last decade. There are also Clean Air Status and Trends Network (CASTNET) dry deposition measurements at Denali and Poker Flats. At all monitored sites in Alaska, wet N deposition has consistently been less than 1 kg N/ha/yr, and it has been less than 0.5 kg N/ha/yr at all monitored sites except Juneau. Wet S deposition has been slightly higher than 1 kg S/ha/yr at Juneau, but less than that at the other monitoring sites. The dry deposition measurements by CASTNET have also been low. Thus, the sparse available atmospheric deposition data for Alaska are consistent with the general understanding that atmospheric deposition of both N and S tends to be very low at national park lands within Alaska. It can be assumed that N and S deposition in each of the Alaskan networks would be lower than 1 to 2 kg/ha/yr, on average.

Land cover in and around the network is shown in Map L. The predominant cover types within this network are forested and perennial ice and snow.

Watershed slope for the parks located in this network is shown on Map M. The slope for most of the park land is between 10° and 20°. SITK has average slope less than 10°, as do small portions of GLBA. Most HUCs in GLBA have average slope between 10° and 20°; there is one small area in GLBA where the slope is steeper, between 20° and 30°.

Park lands requiring special protection against potential adverse impacts associated with acidic deposition are shown on Map N. Also shown on Map N are all federal lands designated as wilderness, both lands managed by NPS and lands managed by other federal agencies. The land designations used to identify this heightened protection included Class I designation under the Clean Air Act Amendments and wilderness designation. There are no Class I areas within this network, but a large percentage of the overall network area is designated wilderness.

Network rankings are given in Figures A through C as the average ranking of the Pollutant Exposure, Ecosystem Sensitivity, and Park Protection metrics, respectively. Figure D shows the overall network Summary Risk ranking. In each figure, the rank for this particular network is highlighted to show its relative position compared with the ranks of the other 31 networks.

The Southeast Alaska Network ranked in the lowest quintile among networks in Pollutant Exposure (Figure A). Emissions and expected deposition of both S and N within the network were very low. The network Ecosystem Sensitivity ranking was also Very Low, within the lowest quintile among networks (Figure B). This network ranked in the top quintile in Park Protection, having substantial amounts of protected lands (Figure C).

In combination, the network rankings for Pollutant Exposure, Ecosystem Sensitivity, and Park Protection yielded an overall Network Risk ranking that is relatively low among networks (Figure D).

Similarly, park rankings are given in Figures E through H for the same metrics. In the case of the park rankings, we only show in the figures the parks that are larger than 100 square miles. Relative ranks for all parks, including the smaller parks, are given in Table A and Appendix A. As for the network ranking figures, the park ranking figures highlight those parks that occur in this network to show their relative position compared with parks in the other 31

networks. Note that the rankings shown in Figures E through H reflect the rank of a given park compared with all other parks, irrespective of size.

All three parks in this network ranked in the lowest quintile for Pollutant Exposure (Figure E, Table A). Ecosystem Sensitivity was ranked in the second highest quintile for GLBA and KLGO, but lower for SITK (Figure F, Table A). GLBA was in the highest quintile in Park Protection (Figure G), whereas the two smaller parks were in the middle quintile for this theme (Table A).

The combined park Summary Risk ranked GLBA as Moderate (Figure H, Table A). The risk for the two smaller parks is considered Moderate for KLGO and Low for SITK (Table A).

Table A. Relative rankings of individual I&M parks within the network for Pollutant Exposure, Ecosystem Sensitivity, Park Protection, and overall Summary Risk from acidic deposition.

I&M Parks[2] in Network	Relative Ranking of Individual Parks[1]			
	Pollutant Exposure	Ecosystem Sensitivity	Park Protection	Summary Risk
Glacier Bay	Very Low	High	Very High	Moderate
Klondike Gold Rush	Very Low	High	Moderate	Moderate
Sitka	Very Low	Low	Moderate	Low

[1] Relative park rankings are designated according to quintile ranking, among all I&M Parks, from the lowest quintile (very low risk) to the highest quintile (very high risk).

[2] Park name is printed in bold italic for parks larger than 100 square miles.

Map A.   National map of total S emissions by county for the year 2002, in units of tons of S per square mile per year. (Source of data: EPA National Emissions Inventory, http://www.epa.gov/ttn/chief/net/2002inventory.html)

Map B.   National map of total N emissions by county for the year 2002. Both oxidized (nitrogen oxides, NO_x) and reduced (ammonia, NH_3) forms of N are included. The total is expressed in tons per square mile per year. (Source of data: EPA National Emissions Inventory, http://www.epa.gov/ttn/chief/net/2002inventory.html)

Map C.   Regional S deposition data are not available for Alaska. Total S deposition throughout most areas in Alaska is expected to be low, below about 1 to 2 kilograms of S per hectare per year. Total S deposition for the continental United States is presented for context here for the year 2002, expressed in units of kilograms of S deposited from the atmosphere to the earth surface per hectare per year. Wet and dry forms of deposition are included. For the eastern half of the country, wet deposition values were derived from interpolated measured values from NADP (three-year average centered on 2002) and dry deposition values were derived from 12-km CMAQ model projections for 2002. For the western half of the country, both wet and dry deposition values were derived from 36-km CMAQ model projections for 2002. NADP interpolations were performed using the approach of Grimm and Lynch (1997). CMAQ model projections were provided by Robin Dennis, U.S. EPA.

Map D.   Regional N deposition data are not available for Alaska. Total N deposition throughout most areas in Alaska is expected to be low, below about 1 to 2 kilograms of N per hectare per year. Total N deposition for the continental United States is presented for context here for the year 2002, expressed in units of kilograms of N deposited from the atmosphere to the earth surface per hectare per year. Wet and dry forms of both oxidized (nitrogen oxides, NO_x) and reduced (ammonia, NH_3) N are included. For the eastern half of the country, wet deposition values were derived from interpolated measured values from NADP (three-year average centered on 2002) and dry deposition values were derived from 12-km CMAQ model projections for 2002. For the western half of the country, both wet and dry deposition values were derived from 36-km CMAQ model projections for 2002. NADP interpolations were performed using the approach of Grimm and Lynch (1997). CMAQ model projections were provided by Robin Dennis, U.S. EPA.

Map E.   Total S emissions by county for lands surrounding the network, expressed as tons of S emitted into the atmosphere per square mile per year. (Source of data: EPA National Emissions Inventory, http://www.epa.gov/ttn/chief/net/2002inventory.html)

Map F.   Total N emissions by county for lands surrounding the network, expressed as tons of N emitted into the atmosphere per square mile per year. The total includes both oxidized (nitrogen oxides, NO_x) and reduced (ammonia, NH_3) N. (Source of data: EPA National Emissions Inventory, http://www.epa.gov/ttn/chief/net/2002inventory.html)

Map G.   Major point source emissions of SO_2 for lands surrounding the network. (Source of data: EPA National Emissions Inventory, http://www.epa.gov/ttn/chief/net/2002inventory.html)

Map H.   Major point source emissions of oxidized (nitrogen oxides, NO_x) and reduced (ammonia, NH_3) N in and around the network. The base of each vertical bar is positioned in the map at the approximate location of the source. The height of the bar is proportional to the magnitude of the source. (Source of data: EPA National Emissions Inventory, http://www.epa.gov/ttn/chief/net/2002inventory.html)

Map I.   Urban centers having more than 10,000 people within the network and within a 300-mile buffer around the perimeter of the network. (Source of data: U.S. Census 2000)

Map L.   Land cover types in and around the network, based on the National Land Cover dataset. (Source of data: National Land Cover Dataset, http://www.mrlc.gov/nlcd_multizone_map.php)

Map M.   Average land slope within park units that occur within the network, by 10-digit HUC. (Source of data: U.S. EPA National Elevation Dataset [http://ned.usgs.gov/])

Map N.   Lands within the network that are classified as Class I or wilderness area. (Source of data: USGS 2005 [National Atlas; http://nationalatlas.gov] and NPS)

Figure A.   Network rankings for Pollutant Exposure, calculated as the average of scores for all Pollutant Exposure variables.

Figure B.   Network rankings for Ecosystem Sensitivity, calculated as the average of scores for all Ecosystem Sensitivity variables.

Figure C.   Network rankings for Park Protection, calculated as the average of scores for all Park Protection variables.

Figure D.   Network Summary Risk rankings, calculated as the average of the quintile ranks for the Pollutant Exposure, Ecosystem Sensitivity, and Park Protection themes.

Figure E. Park rankings for Pollutant Exposure for all parks larger than 100 square miles. Ranks for each park were calculated relative to all parks, regardless of size, as the average of scores for all Pollutant Exposure variables.

Figure F. Park rankings for Ecosystem Sensitivity for all parks larger than 100 square miles. Ranks for each park were calculated relative to all parks, regardless of size, as the average of scores for all Ecosystem Sensitivity variables.

Figure G. Park rankings for Park Protection for all parks larger than 100 square miles. Ranks for each park were calculated relative to all parks, regardless of size, as the average of scores for all Park Protection variables.

Figure H. Park rankings for Summary Risk for all parks larger than 100 square miles. Ranks for each park were calculated relative to all parks, regardless of size, as the average of the quintile ranks for the Pollutant Exposure, Ecosystem Sensitivity, and Park Protection themes.

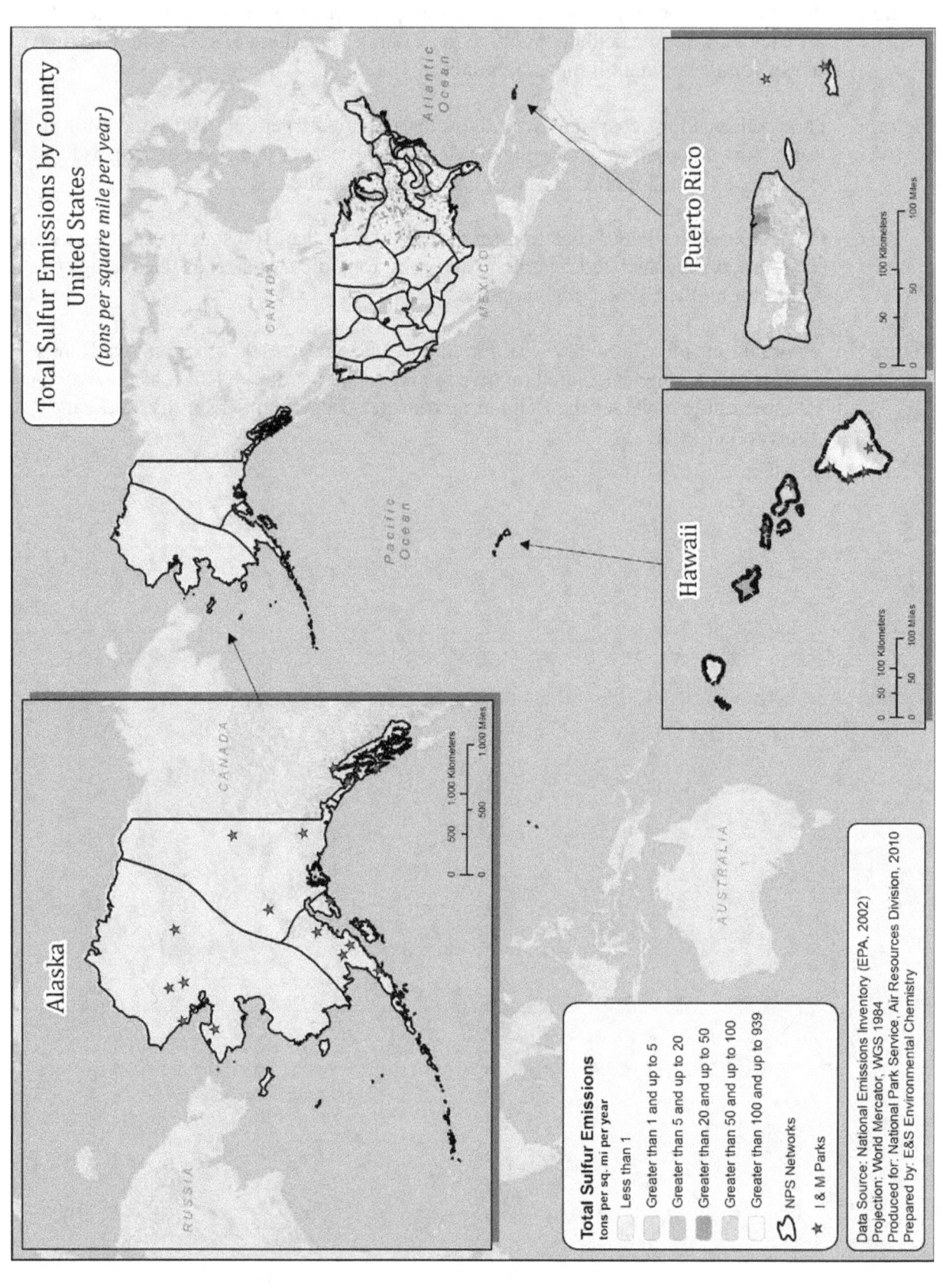

Total Sulfur Emissions by County
United States
(tons per square mile per year)

Total Sulfur Emissions
tons per sq. mi per year

Less than 1
Greater than 1 and up to 5
Greater than 5 and up to 20
Greater than 20 and up to 50
Greater than 50 and up to 100
Greater than 100 and up to 939

NPS Networks
I & M Parks

Data Source: National Emissions Inventory (EPA, 2002)
Projection: World Mercator, WGS 1984
Produced for: National Park Service, Air Resources Division, 2010
Prepared by: E&S Environmental Chemistry

Map A

Total Nitrogen Emissions by County
United States
(tons per square mile per year)

Alaska

Puerto Rico

Hawaii

Total Nitrogen Emissions
tons per sq. mi per year
Less than 1
Greater than 1 and up to 5
Greater than 5 and up to 20
Greater than 20 and up to 50
Greater than 50 and up to 100
Greater than 100 and up to 618
NPS Networks
I & M Parks

Data Source: National Emissions Inventory (EPA, 2002)
Projection: World Mercator, WGS 1984
Produced for: National Park Service, Air Resources Division, 2010
Prepared by: E&S Environmental Chemistry

Map B

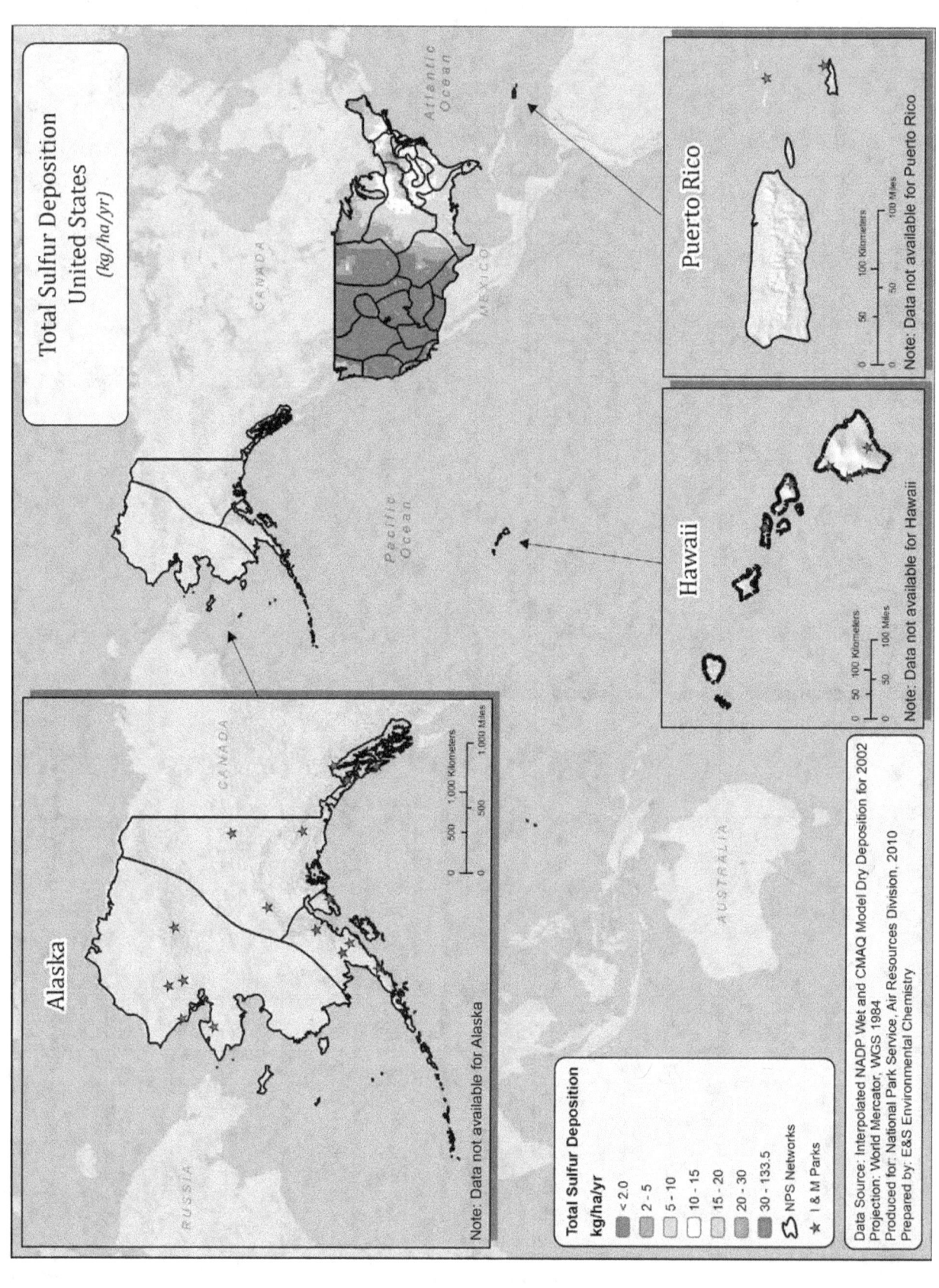

Total Sulfur Deposition
United States
[kg/ha/yr]

Alaska

Note: Data not available for Alaska

| 0 | 500 | 1,000 Kilometers |
| 0 | 500 | 1,000 Miles |

Hawaii

Note: Data not available for Hawaii

| 0 | 50 | 100 Kilometers |
| 0 | 50 | 100 Miles |

Puerto Rico

Note: Data not available for Puerto Rico

| 0 | 50 | 100 Kilometers |
| 0 | 50 | 100 Miles |

Total Sulfur Deposition
kg/ha/yr
- < 2.0
- 2 - 5
- 5 - 10
- 10 - 15
- 15 - 20
- 20 - 30
- 30 - 133.5
- NPS Networks
- ★ I & M Parks

Data Source: Interpolated NADP Wet and CMAQ Model Dry Deposition for 2002
Projection: World Mercator, WGS 1984
Produced for: National Park Service, Air Resources Division, 2010
Prepared by: E&S Environmental Chemistry

Map C

SEAN-8

Total Nitrogen Deposition
United States
(kg/ha/yr)

Atlantic Ocean

CANADA

MEXICO

RUSSIA

CANADA

Pacific Ocean

AUSTRALIA

Alaska

Note: Data not available for Alaska

0   500   1,000 Kilometers

0   500   1,000 Miles

Hawaii

Note: Data not available for Hawaii

0   50   100 Kilometers

0   50   100 Miles

Puerto Rico

Note: Data not available for Puerto Rico

0   50   100 Kilometers

0   50   100 Miles

Total Nitrogen Deposition
kg/ha/yr
< 2.0
2 - 5
5 - 10
10 - 15
15 - 20
20 - 30
30 - 63.5
NPS Networks
★ I & M Parks

Data Source: Interpolated NADP Wet and CMAQ Model Dry Deposition for 2002
Projection: World Mercator, WGS 1984
Produced for: National Park Service, Air Resources Division, 2010
Prepared by: E&S Environmental Chemistry

Map D

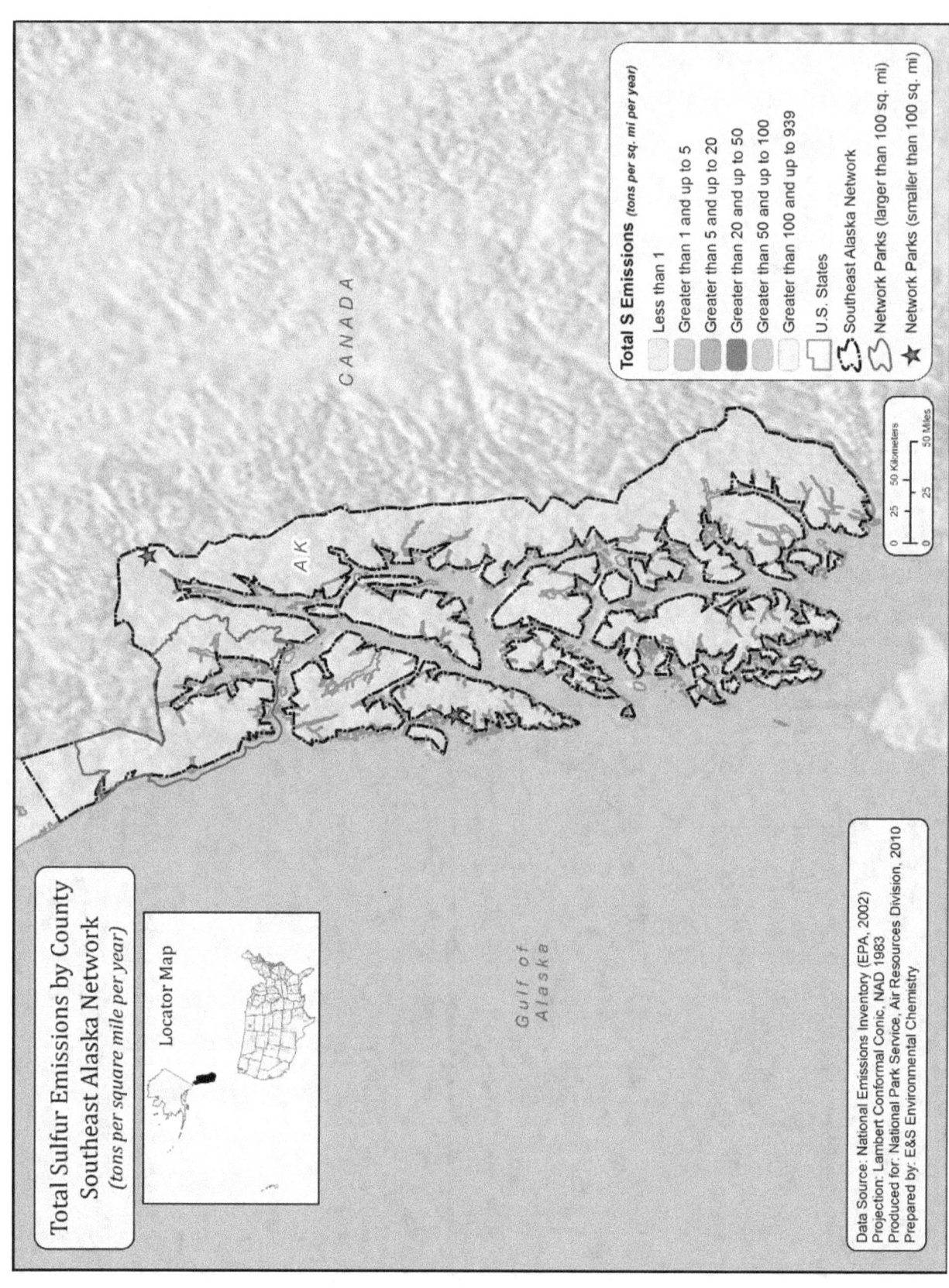

Total Sulfur Emissions by County
Southeast Alaska Network
(tons per square mile per year)

Locator Map

Total S Emissions *(tons per sq. mi per year)*

- Less than 1
- Greater than 1 and up to 5
- Greater than 5 and up to 20
- Greater than 20 and up to 50
- Greater than 50 and up to 100
- Greater than 100 and up to 939
- U.S. States
- Southeast Alaska Network
- Network Parks (larger than 100 sq. mi)
- ★ Network Parks (smaller than 100 sq. mi)

CANADA

A K

Gulf of Alaska

0   25   50 Kilometers
0   25   50 Miles

Data Source: National Emissions Inventory (EPA, 2002)
Projection: Lambert Conformal Conic, NAD 1983
Produced for: National Park Service, Air Resources Division, 2010
Prepared by: E&S Environmental Chemistry

Map E

Total Nitrogen Emissions by County
Southeast Alaska Network
(tons per square mile per year)

Locator Map

Gulf of
Alaska

CANADA

AK

Total N Emissions *(tons per sq. mi per year)*

Less than 1
Greater than 1 and up to 5
Greater than 5 and up to 20
Greater than 20 and up to 50
Greater than 50 and up to 100
Greater than 100 and up to 618
U.S. States
Southeast Alaska Network
Network Parks (larger than 100 sq. mi)
Network Parks (smaller than 100 sq. mi)

0 25 50 Kilometers
0 25 50 Miles

Data Source: National Emissions Inventory (EPA, 2002)
Projection: Lambert Conformal Conic, NAD 1983
Produced for: National Park Service, Air Resources Division, 2010
Prepared by: E&S Environmental Chemistry

Map F

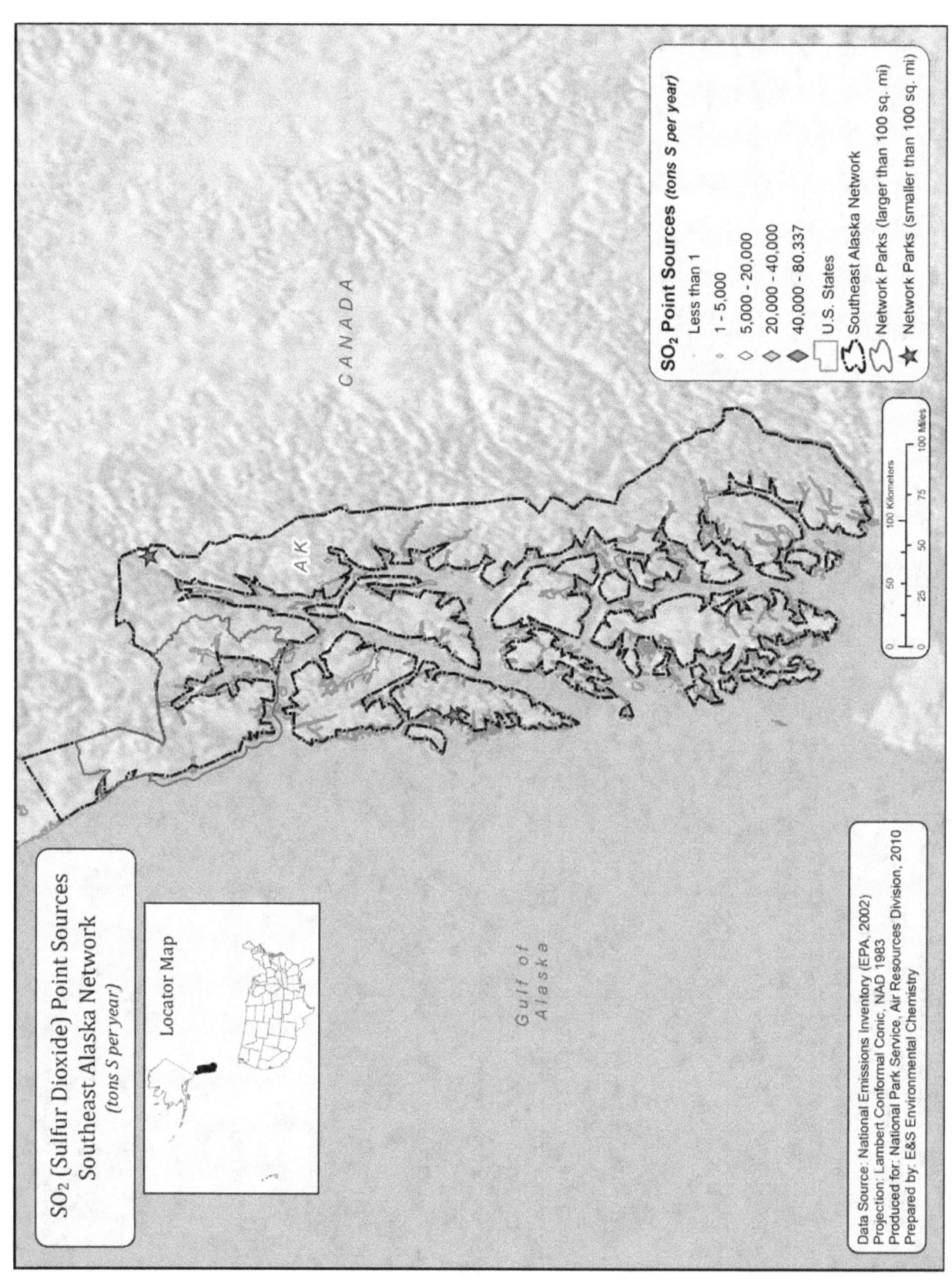

SO₂ (Sulfur Dioxide) Point Sources
Southeast Alaska Network
(tons S per year)

Locator Map

SO₂ Point Sources (tons S per year)

- Less than 1
- 1 - 5,000
- 5,000 - 20,000
- 20,000 - 40,000
- 40,000 - 80,337

U.S. States

Southeast Alaska Network

Network Parks (larger than 100 sq. mi)

Network Parks (smaller than 100 sq. mi)

CANADA

AK

Gulf of Alaska

100 Kilometers
100 Miles

Data Source: National Emissions Inventory (EPA, 2002)
Projection: Lambert Conformal Conic, NAD 1983
Produced for: National Park Service, Air Resources Division, 2010
Prepared by: E&S Environmental Chemistry

Map G

NO$_x$ (Nitrogen Oxides) and NH$_3$ (Ammonia) Point Sources
Southeast Alaska Network
(tons N per year)

Locator Map

CANADA

Gulf of
Alaska

NO$_x$ Point Sources *(tons N per year)*
— 2,500 tons N/year

NH$_3$ Point Sources *(tons N per year)*
— 1,000 tons N/year

☐ U.S. States
⌇ Southeast Alaska Network
⌘ Network Parks (larger than 100 sq. mi)
★ Network Parks (smaller than 100 sq. mi)

0   25   50   75   100 Miles
0   50   100 Kilometers

Data Source: National Emissions Inventory (EPA, 2002)
Projection: Lambert Conformal Conic, NAD 1983
Produced for: National Park Service, Air Resources Division, 2010
Prepared by: E&S Environmental Chemistry

Map H

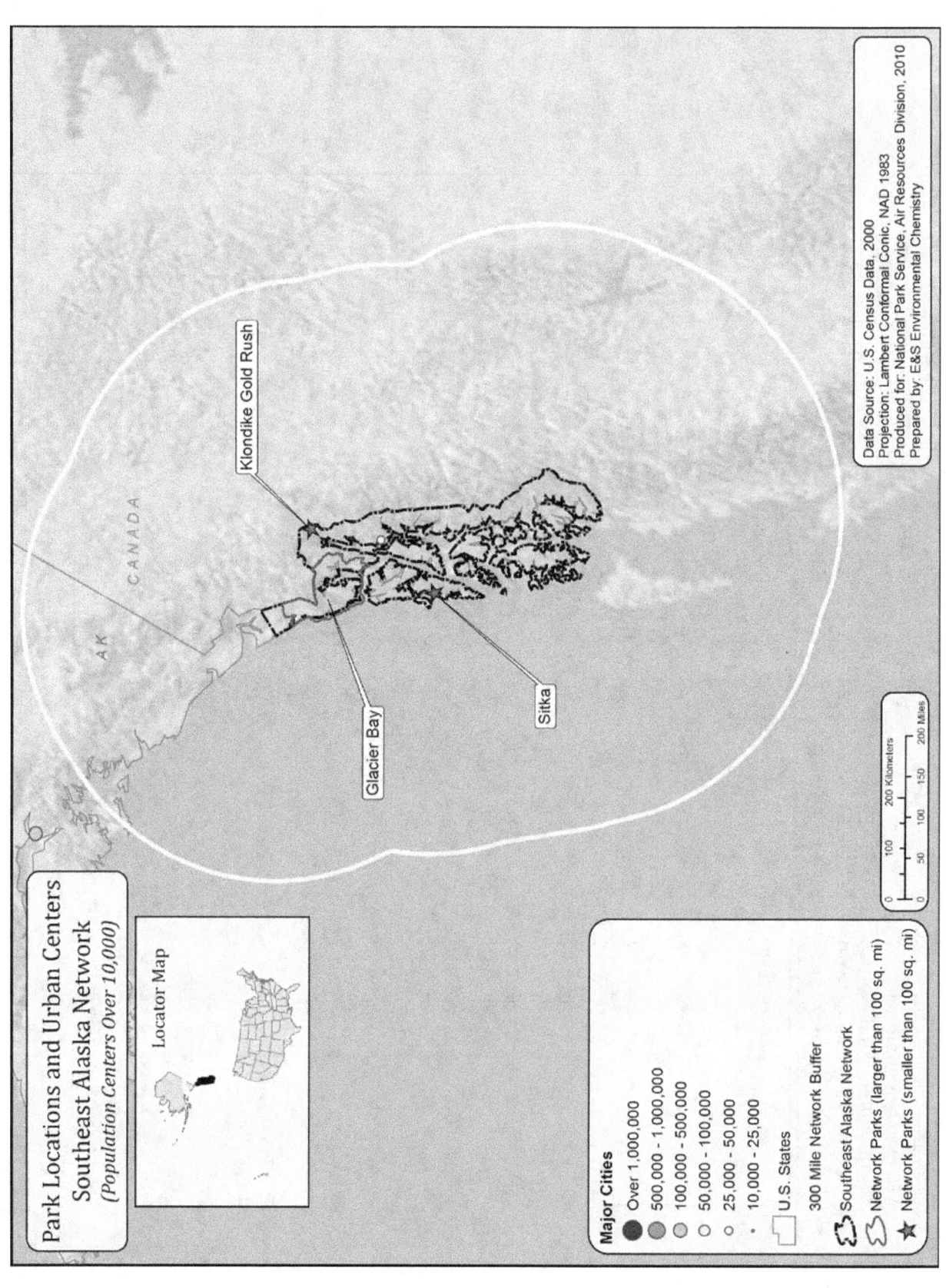

Park Locations and Urban Centers
Southeast Alaska Network
(Population Centers Over 10,000)

Locator Map

Major Cities

●	Over 1,000,000
●	500,000 - 1,000,000
●	100,000 - 500,000
○	50,000 - 100,000
○	25,000 - 50,000
·	10,000 - 25,000

U.S. States

300 Mile Network Buffer

Southeast Alaska Network

Network Parks (larger than 100 sq. mi)

★ Network Parks (smaller than 100 sq. mi)

Klondike Gold Rush

Glacier Bay

Sitka

CANADA

AK

Data Source: U.S. Census Data, 2000
Projection: Lambert Conformal Conic, NAD 1983
Produced for: National Park Service, Air Resources Division, 2010
Prepared by: E&S Environmental Chemistry

0 50 100 150 200 Miles
0 100 200 Kilometers

Map I

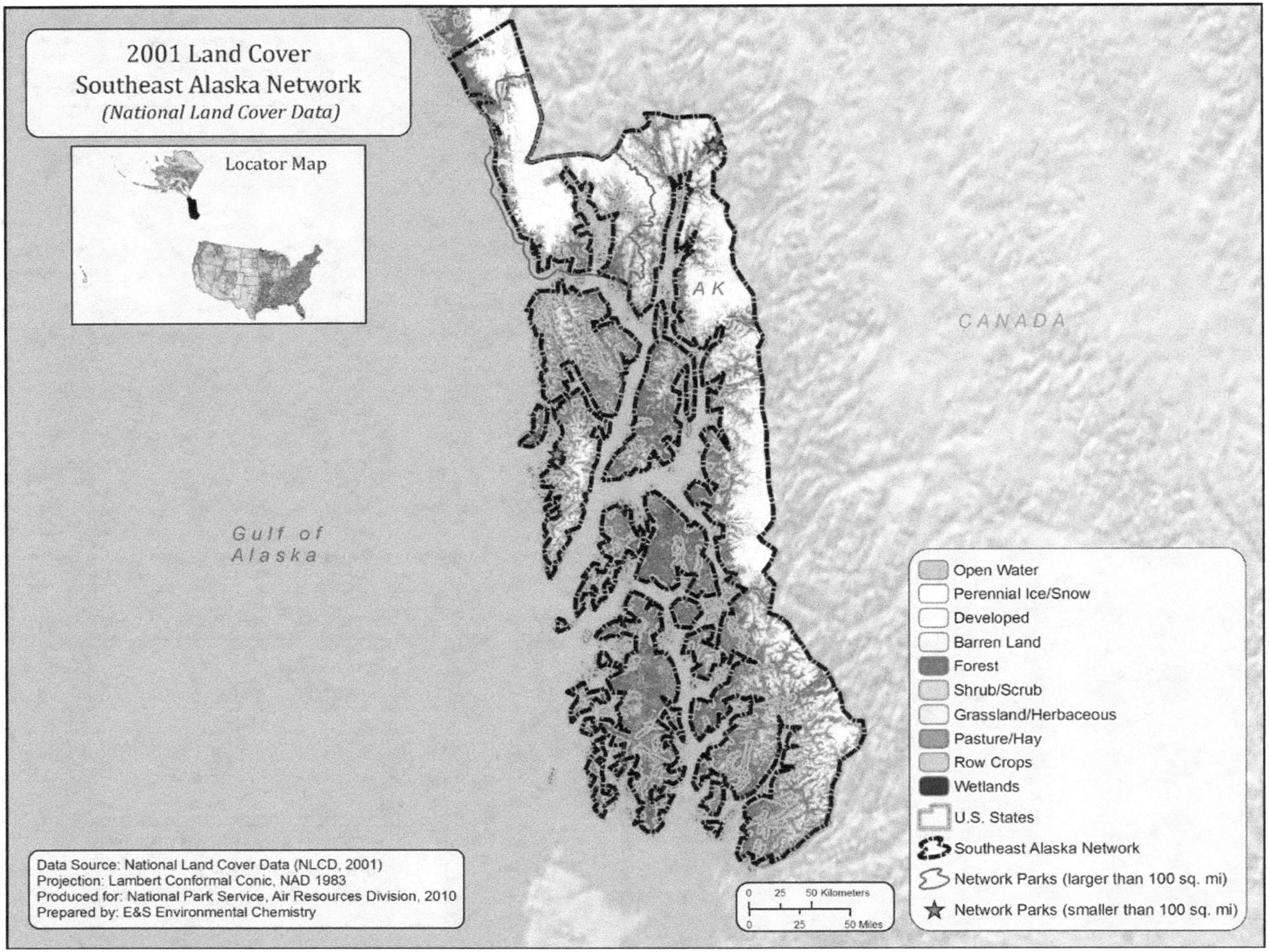

2001 Land Cover
Southeast Alaska Network
(National Land Cover Data)

Locator Map

Legend

- Open Water
- Perennial Ice/Snow
- Developed
- Barren Land
- Forest
- Shrub/Scrub
- Grassland/Herbaceous
- Pasture/Hay
- Row Crops
- Wetlands
- U.S. States
- Southeast Alaska Network
- Network Parks (larger than 100 sq. mi)
- Network Parks (smaller than 100 sq. mi)

CANADA

A K

Gulf of Alaska

0 25 50 Kilometers
0 25 50 Miles

Data Source: National Land Cover Data (NLCD, 2001)
Projection: Lambert Conformal Conic, NAD 1983
Produced for: National Park Service, Air Resources Division, 2010
Prepared by: E&S Environmental Chemistry

Map L

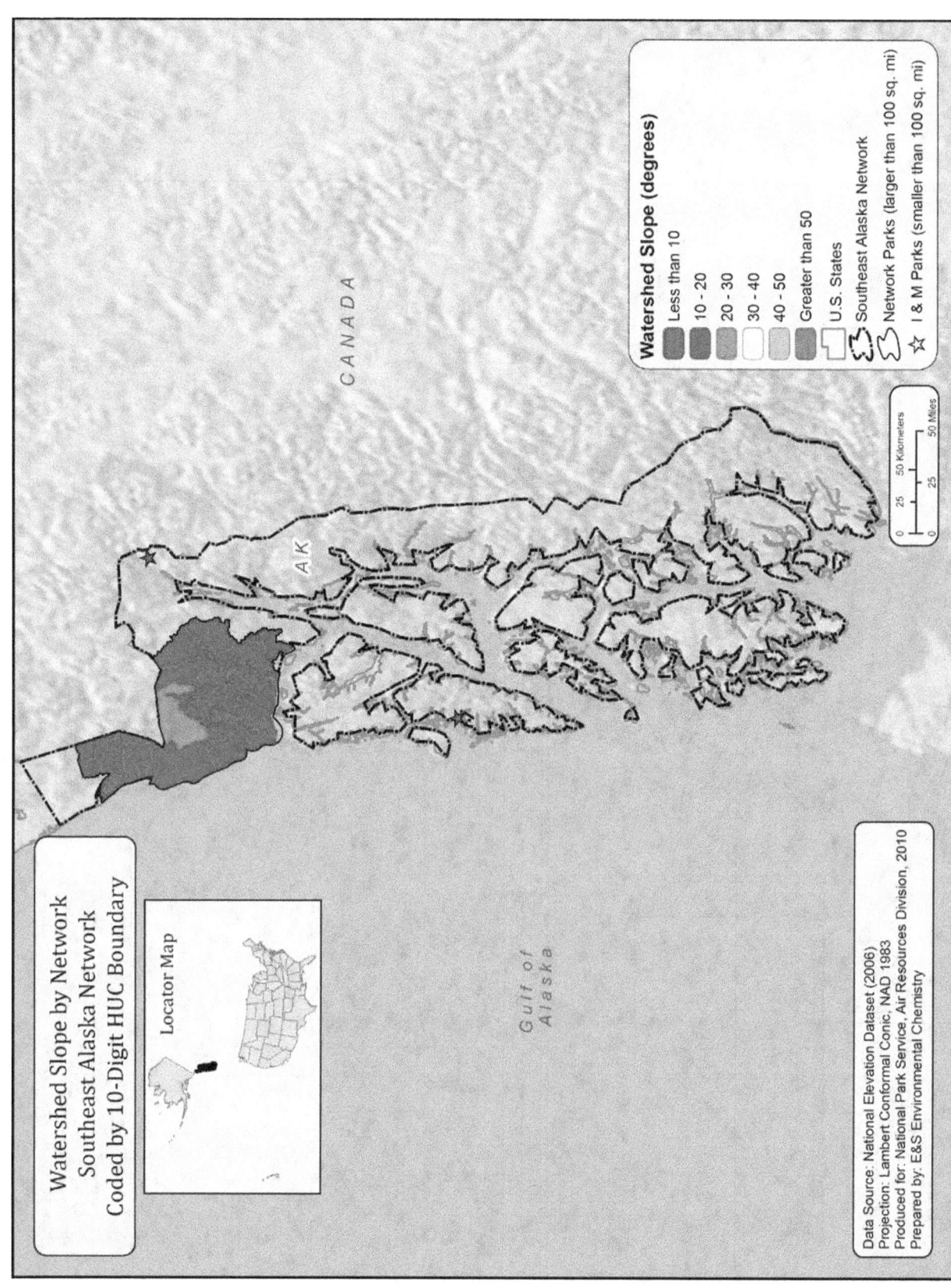

Watershed Slope by Network
Southeast Alaska Network
Coded by 10-Digit HUC Boundary

Locator Map

CANADA

AK

Gulf of
Alaska

Watershed Slope (degrees)

Less than 10
10 - 20
20 - 30
30 - 40
40 - 50
Greater than 50
U.S. States
Southeast Alaska Network
Network Parks (larger than 100 sq. mi)
I & M Parks (smaller than 100 sq. mi)

0   25   50 Kilometers
0   25   50 Miles

Data Source: National Elevation Dataset (2006)
Projection: Lambert Conformal Conic, NAD 1983
Produced for: National Park Service, Air Resources Division, 2010
Prepared by: E&S Environmental Chemistry

Map M

Class I and Wilderness Areas
Southeast Alaska Network

Locator Map

CANADA

AK

Gulf of
Alaska

Class I and Wilderness Areas

Wilderness
NPS Class I
NPS Class I and Wilderness Overlap
U.S. States
Southeast Alaska Network
Network Parks (larger than 100 sq. mi)
★ Network Parks (smaller than 100 sq. mi)

0   25   50 Kilometers
0   25   50 Miles

Data Source: National Park Service (2007) and National Atlas (2005)
Projection: Lambert Conformal Conic, NAD 1983
Produced for: National Park Service, Air Resources Division, 2010
Prepared by: E&S Environmental Chemistry

Map N

Figure A

Acidification Risk Assessment
Ecosystem Sensitivity Ranking

Figure B

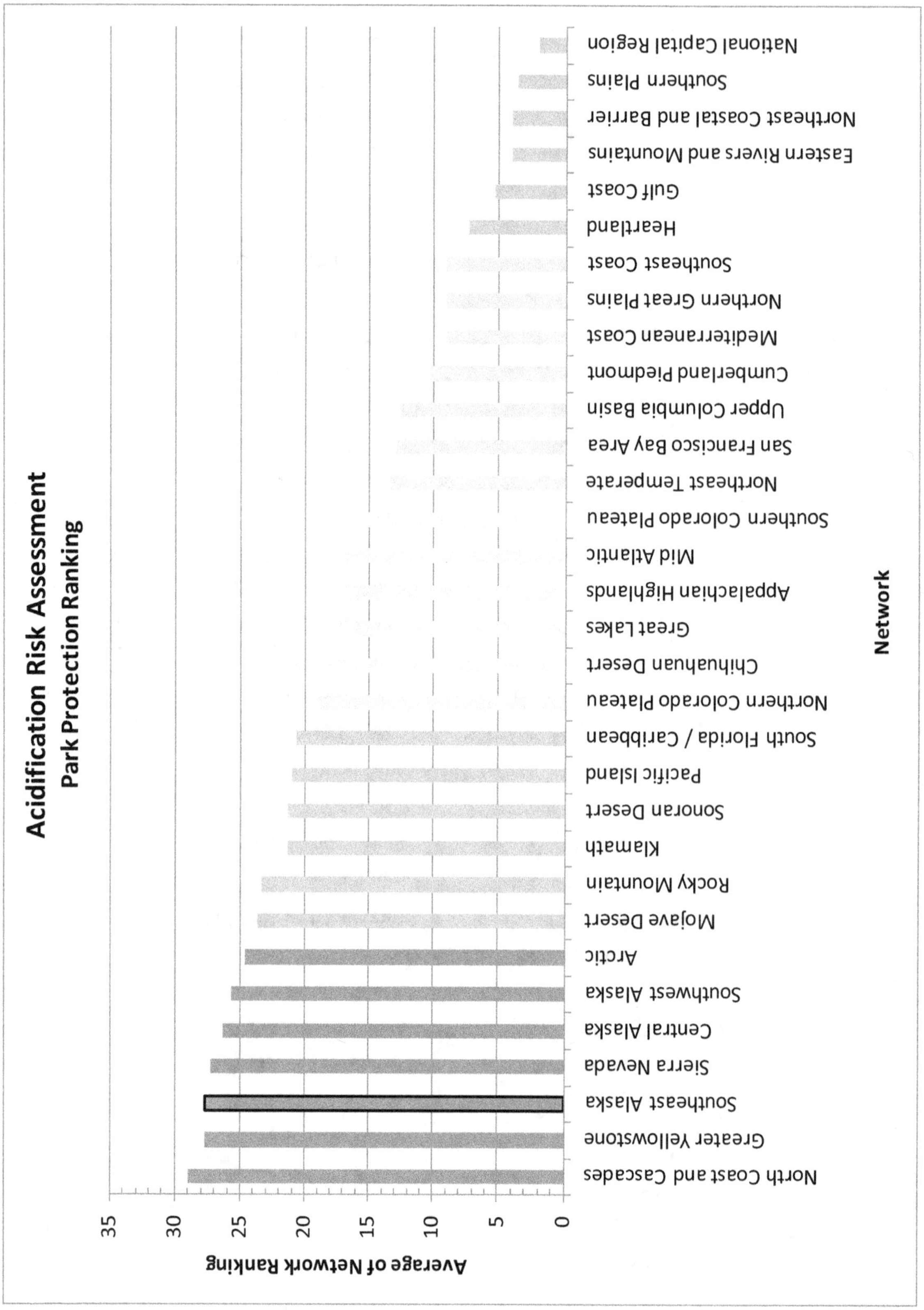
Acidification Risk Assessment
Park Protection Ranking
Average of Network Ranking
0
5
10
15
20
25
30
35
Network
North Coast and Cascades
Greater Yellowstone
Southeast Alaska
Sierra Nevada
Central Alaska
Southwest Alaska
Arctic
Mojave Desert
Rocky Mountain
Klamath
Sonoran Desert
Pacific Island
South Florida / Caribbean
Northern Colorado Plateau
Chihuahuan Desert
Great Lakes
Appalachian Highlands
Mid Atlantic
Southern Colorado Plateau
Northeast Temperate
San Francisco Bay Area
Upper Columbia Basin
Cumberland Piedmont
Mediterranean Coast
Northern Great Plains
Southeast Coast
Heartland
Gulf Coast
Eastern Rivers and Mountains
Northeast Coastal and Barrier
Southern Plains
National Capital Region

Figure C

Figure D

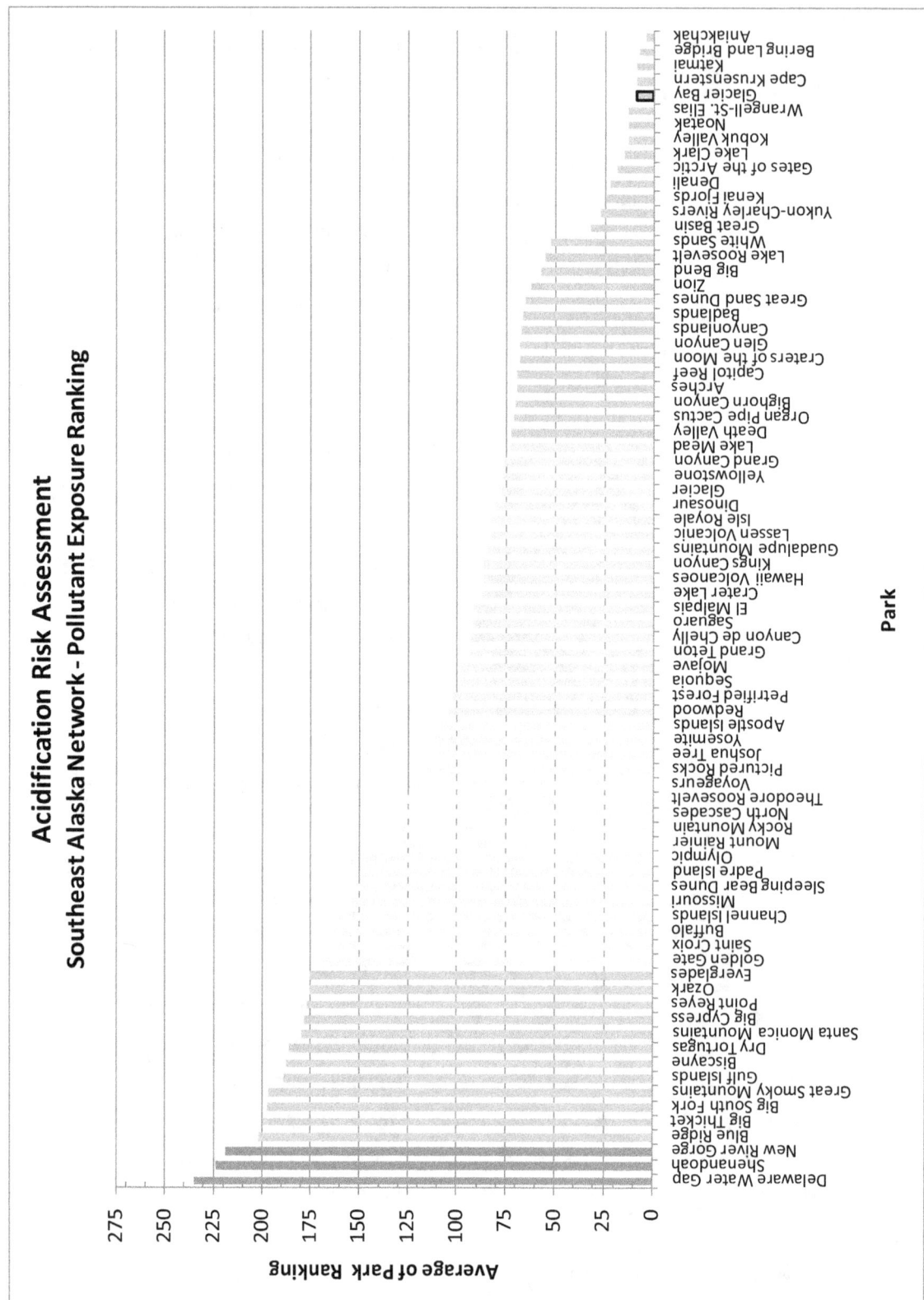

Figure E

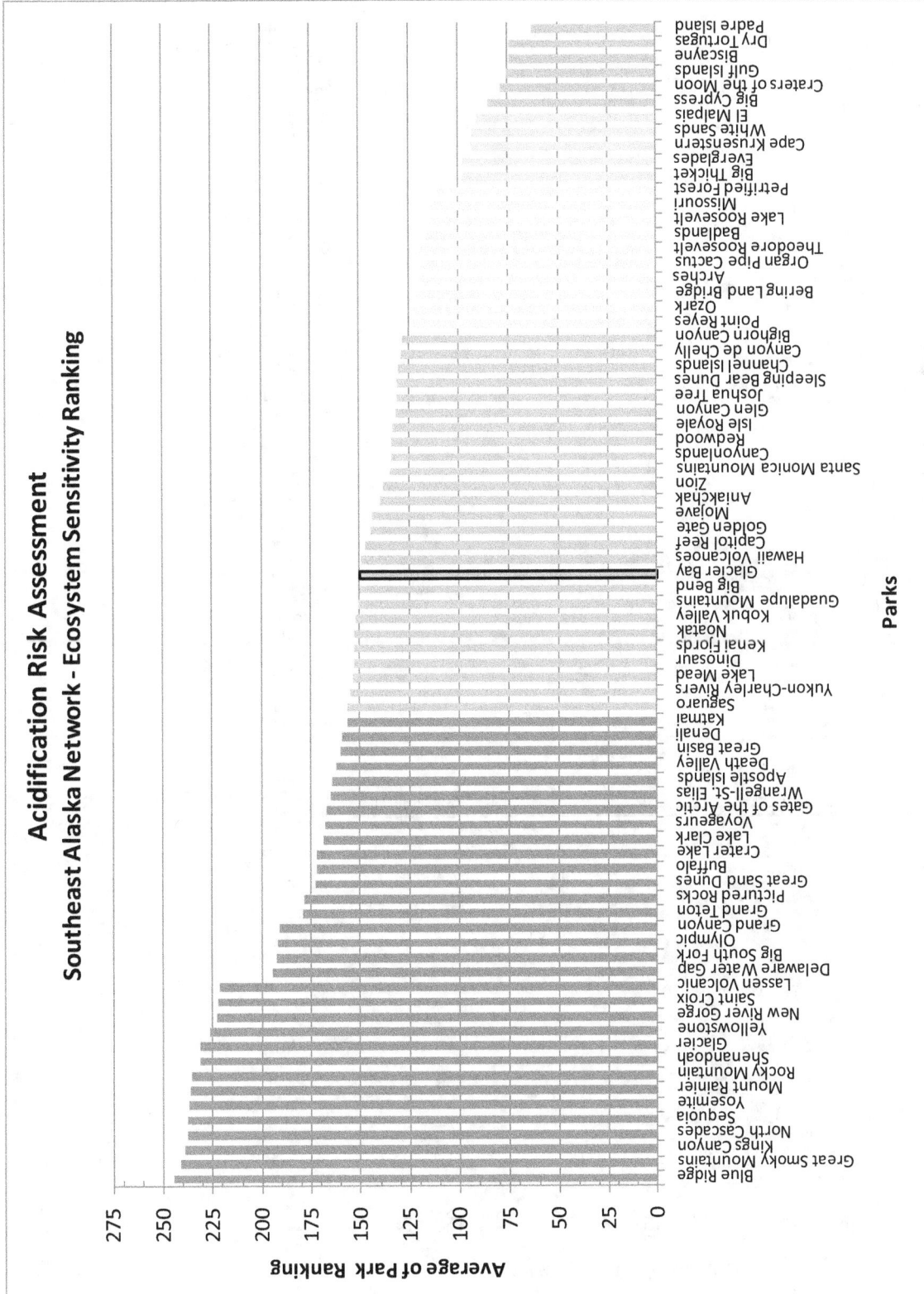

Figure F

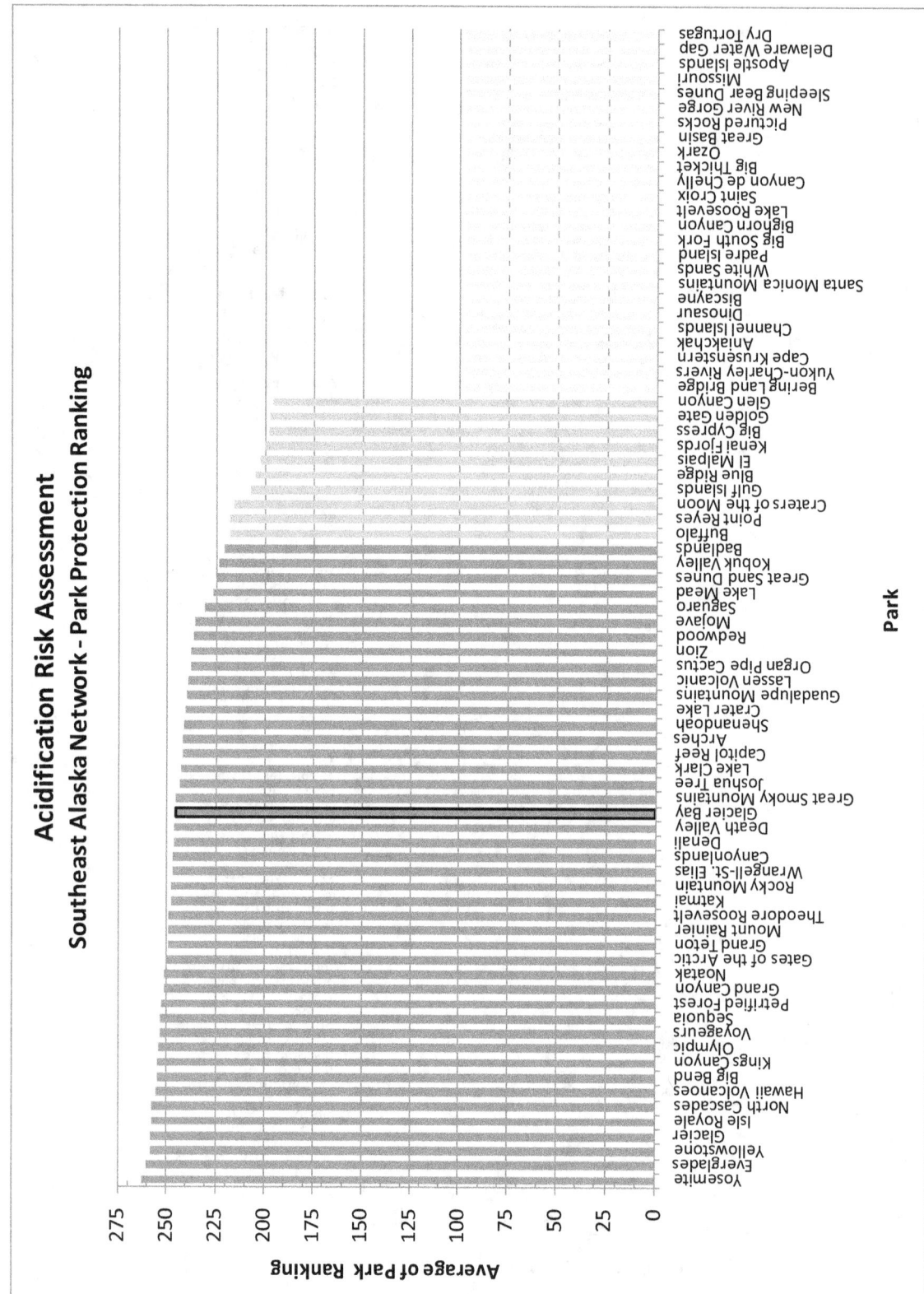

Figure G

Acidification Risk Assessment

Southeast Alaska Network – Summary Risk Ranking

Figure H

The Department of the Interior protects and manages the nation's natural resources and cultural heritage; provides scientific and other information about those resources; and honors its special responsibilities to American Indians, Alaska Natives, and affiliated Island Communities.

NPS 953/107409, April 2011

National Park Service
U.S. Department of the Interior

Natural Resource Program Center
Air Resources Division
PO Box 25287
Denver, CO 80225

www.nature.nps.gov/air

EXPERIENCE YOUR AMERICA ™

www.ingramcontent.com/pod-product-compliance
Lightning Source LLC
Chambersburg PA
CBHW080938290526
45795CB00007BA/2813